Revise WJEC GCSE English Literature

DRAMA　　　　poetry　　　　FORM

interpretation

response　　　language

context

PROSE　　　　　COMPARISON

Roger Lane

Consultants
Margaret Graham
Ken Welsh

WJEC CBAC

OXFORD
UNIVERSITY PRESS

OXFORD
UNIVERSITY PRESS

Great Clarendon Street, Oxford OX2 6DP

Oxford University Press is a department of the University of Oxford.
It furthers the University's objective of excellence in research,
scholarship, and education by publishing worldwide in

Oxford   New York

Auckland   Cape Town   Dar es Salaam   Hong Kong   Karachi
Kuala Lumpur   Madrid   Melbourne   Mexico City   Nairobi
New Delhi   Shanghai   Taipei   Toronto

With offices in

Argentina   Austria   Brazil   Chile   Czech Republic   France   Greece
Guatemala   Hungary   Italy   Japan   Poland   Portugal   Singapore
South Korea   Switzerland   Thailand   Turkey   Ukraine   Vietnam

Oxford is a registered trade mark of Oxford University Press
in the UK and in certain other countries

British Library Cataloguing in Publication Data

Data available

ISBN 13: 978 0 19 831885 9
ISBN 10: 0 19 831885 5

3 5 7 9 10 8 6 4

Designed and typeset by Mike Brain Graphic Design Limited

Printed in Spain by Unigraf

Acknowledgements

The author would like to thank:
Hugh Lester – for generous help and support, and
Elizabeth Evans – for yet more sample answers.

Thanks also for the work on mind maps to Caroline Youds and
Catherine Millanof Plessington Catholic High School, Bebington, Wirral.

We are grateful for permission to include the
following copyright material in this book:
Roddy Doyle: Extract from *Paddy Clarke Ha Ha Ha*
(Secker & Warburg, 1993), reprinted by permission of
The Random House Group Limited.
John Idris Jones: 'First Day' and 'Elvis Presley' both from
Renewals: Selected Poems 1958–1998 (Conybeare Publishing, 1999),
reprinted by permission of the author.
Harper Lee: Extract from *To Kill a Mockingbird* (Heinemann, 1960),
reprinted by permission of The Random House Group Limited.
Dylan Thomas: Extract from 'The Extraordinary Little Cough'
taken from *Collected Stories* (Orion, 1983), reprinted by permission
of David Higham Associates Ltd.

Although we have tried to trace and contact copyright holders before
publication, in some cases this has not been possible. If notified we will be
pleased to rectify any errors or omissions at the earliest opportunity.

This book is dedicated to the memory of Wyn Roberts

Contents

To the student

This guide helps to prepare you for the GCSE examination paper at the end of your WJEC English Literature course. It does this by familiarising you with each aspect of the exam, the skills and approaches you need to adopt, and the types of questions you will be asked. The guide encourages you to make the most of your knowledge and understanding of your set books by organising yourself and feeling confident about your own personal response.

This guide works alongside the Oxford/WJEC *Students' Book*, *Teacher's Guide* and *Coursework Guide*, but it should help you perfectly well if you use it as a 'stand-alone' revision aid without any reference to the other titles. It should help whether you are reading it just days before your exams or with a few months to prepare. You should find that it works without the intervention of your teacher, tutor or parents, although none of them are banned from reading it!

The first page asks you to decide which Specification you are following. It then maps out the GCSE English Literature course to show where the final exams fit into it. GCSE English will almost certainly feature both as another qualification and also as an overlap with English Literature (especially in coursework). There is a separate *GCSE English Revision Guide*.

The sample answers in this guide are all quite impressive, not to frighten you, nor to make you feel inadequate, but to make you aware of what is possible in response to the questions and tasks set. (The *Teacher's Guide* contains many sample answers showing work at a range of different grades.) Candidates do display remarkable quality under examination conditions and also manage to sustain it at some length. Generally, the sample answers go beyond what is required for full marks!

The best way to use this guide would be to follow the advice for organising your reading and note-taking, then to answer at least one specimen question from each section of your exam (either Specification A or Specification B) before studying the sample responses. However, reading the guide and simply taking in the advice might be the most useful approach if your exams are approaching very soon. Whichever approach you adopt, all the very best of luck in the 'real thing' – remember to keep calm, use the time fully and concentrate on giving your best possible performance. You might be better than you imagine. Good luck!

Roger Lane

ROGER LANE

How the exams fit into the GCSE English Literature course

Are you studying WJEC Specification A or WJEC Specification B? Highlight the heading of your Specification below.

Specification A (Foundation/Higher)

Coursework (four pieces for assessment; 30% of total assessment)

1. Poetry (pre-1914)
2. Poetry (post-1914)
3. Prose
4. Drama

Pre- and post-1914 prose and drama must be covered across coursework and the examination. At least two assignments must compare texts. One piece must be teacher supervised. At least one piece must be handwritten.

Examination (one paper; 2 hours 30 minutes; 70% of total assessment)

Section A (about one hour)
Set text – prose: answer question(s) on an extract; extended writing on a set text
Section B (about one hour)
Set text – drama: answer question(s) on an extract; extended writing on a set text
Section C (about 30 minutes)
Poetry: guided response to an unseen poem

Specification B (Foundation/Higher)

The distinctive features of Specification B are:

- ♠ you will complete a 'wider reading' piece of coursework
- ♠ you will answer questions on 'comparing texts' in the exam
- ♠ you will study the WJEC Anthology (containing prose and poetry) for the literature exam.

Coursework (four pieces for assessment; 30% of total assessment)

1. Poetry (pre-1914)
2. Prose (pre-1914)
3. Drama
4. Wider reading

Pre- and post-1914 drama must be covered across coursework and the examination. The WJEC set anthology for Specification B covers post-1914 poetry and prose for the examination. Comparison takes place in the examination. 'Wider reading' can be based on poetry, prose or drama, either pre- or post-1914. One piece must be teacher supervised. At least one piece must be handwritten.

Examination (one paper; 2 hours 30 minutes; 70% of total assessment)

Section A (about 55 minutes)
Prose anthology: answer question(s) on an extract; extended writing on the anthology
Section B (about 55 minutes)
Poetry anthology: answer question(s) on an extract; extended writing on the anthology
Section C (about 40 minutes)
Drama: extended writing on a set text

Explaining the small print

What does the English Literature exam expect from you?

- ♠ You must show that you know and understand your set texts.
- ♠ You should look closely at details of language and the way a text is organised and constructed.
- ♠ You should write your answers in a clear and organised way.
- ♠ You should try to show how a text fits into the background of the writer and its historical background.
- ♠ In the Specification B exam, you should show that you can make comparisons between poems and between prose extracts. (If you are doing Specification A, comparing texts is needed in two of your coursework assignments instead.)

Place a tick, a cross or a question mark against each of the points above, according to whether or not you understand what each of them requires. (Each of these points is dealt with fully later in this guide.)

Set prose and drama texts for the exam

For the Literature exam, Specification A candidates will study one text from each of the lists below. Specification B candidates will study one text from the drama section. Highlight the text(s) that you are studying for the exam.

Prose (Specification A only)

2004–5	2006
Charles Dickens, *Hard Times*	**Jane Austen, *Pride and Prejudice***
Roddy Doyle, *Paddy Clarke Ha Ha Ha*	Roddy Doyle, *Paddy Clarke Ha Ha Ha*
George Eliot, *Silas Marner*	George Eliot, *Silas Marner*
Harper Lee, *To Kill a Mockingbird*	Harper Lee, *To Kill a Mockingbird*
John Steinbeck, *Of Mice and Men*	John Steinbeck, *Of Mice and Men*
Robert Swindells, *Stone Cold*	Robert Swindells, *Stone Cold*
Meera Syal, *Anita and Me*	Meera Syal, *Anita and Me*
Maya Angelou, *I Know Why The Caged Bird Sings*	Maya Angelou, *I Know Why The Caged Bird Sings*

Drama (Specification A and Specification B)

2004–5	2006
Harold Brighouse, *Hobson's Choice*	Harold Brighouse, *Hobson's Choice*
Arthur Miller, *A View From The Bridge*	Arthur Miller, *A View From The Bridge*
J.B. Priestley, *An Inspector Calls*	J.B. Priestley, *An Inspector Calls*
Willy Russell, *Blood Brothers*	Willy Russell, *Blood Brothers*
William Shakespeare, *The Merchant of Venice*	William Shakespeare, *The Merchant of Venice*
William Shakespeare, *Romeo and Juliet*	William Shakespeare, *Romeo and Juliet*
William Shakespeare, *The Tempest*	**William Shakespeare, *Othello***
Dylan Thomas, *Under Milk Wood*	Dylan Thomas, *Under Milk Wood*

Approaching the English Literature course

If you are at (or near) the start of your one-year or two-year course, you should make the most of your opportunities in coursework assignments. Do your very best on each piece of coursework first time around, because you will save huge amounts of time later if you do.

Your coursework assignments will offer you chances to answer the same kind of question and practise the same skills as the examination. Even though you will be writing about different texts in coursework, you should try to sharpen your performance as you go through the course. **Take the following advice in coursework as well as in the exam.**

- **Start your response purposefully, not with a loose, vague introduction, nor a lengthy account of the writer's life.**
- **Do not pad out your writing with chunky quotations just to fill the page.**
- **Do not write coursework essays beyond four or five sides of A4 paper.**

In coursework, there may well be an element of re-drafting needed for some of your assignments, but do not make any more of this than is necessary. A second draft is sound practice only when you have something significant to amend, preferably something prompted by your own critical reading of the first draft. See drafting as part of the learning process for the exam – the day that you will have no time to re-draft.

Reading a text independently

You will be a much stronger English Literature exam candidate if you are able and willing to read and study your texts at home. If you do get to read them independently before your teacher introduces them in class, be confident that your reactions to the story will be relevant and useful for later. Answering the following questions as you read will help you become an active reader and a thorough student.

The plot
- What happens at the start? What do you think of the opening?
- How do you expect the story to develop? What are the key stages of the story?
- How do you expect the story to end? What do you think of the ending?
- Are there any questions left unanswered at the end?

The characters
- How important is each character in the story?
- How do some of the characters change as the story develops?
- Are there any moments when you feel strongly for or against particular characters?
- Do the different locations/settings of the story cause the characters to behave differently?

Key scenes and events
- What happens during each of the key scenes or events? Why is each one important?
- How do the main characters behave before and after these key scenes/events?
- Do your opinions of any of the characters change because of any of these scenes or events?

Themes
- What are the main themes and how do they develop?
- How do the main characters demonstrate these themes in their behaviour?
- What is the writer trying to say about these themes?

Mood and atmosphere

- ♣ What is the mood and atmosphere like at the start of the story?
- ♣ How does the mood and atmosphere change, if at all, during the story?
- ♣ What effect do the different settings or locations have on the mood and atmosphere?
- ♣ How does the audience or reader react to the changes in mood and atmosphere?

The writer

- ♣ Do you notice anything that stands out about the writer's style of writing?
- ♣ Is there anything interesting about the way the writer has organised the story?

Approaching the revision of set texts

When you come to re-read your texts in the weeks leading up to the final exam, you need to take a very different approach to that of your initial reading. It is easy to think that you have forgotten everything, and easy to be tempted to re-start the whole reading process. Unfortunately, you probably do not have enough time (bearing in mind your other subjects) and, in any case, **your real task now is pull everything tightly into shape for answering questions in limited periods of time.** Leisurely bedtime reading is not the name of the game! If you start reading from the first line again, there is a real possibility that each time you sit down to read you will slip further behind your target.

Instead, **divide your text(s) into a manageable number of sections.** Perhaps the standard measure would be a Shakespeare play with its five acts, which would allow you five revision sessions on successive days to 're-visit' the whole play. When you settle down to revise the first act, go straight to the end of it, work out where you are in terms of the action at this point and, in manageable steps, track the plot through by flicking back and forth through the pages of Act 1. Using any time available for this first session, look at the characters, themes, settings, etc. that emerge in the early part of the play. Next time, do the same with Act 2, by locating its end, and so on.

In the case of a play with less than five acts, you can complete the coverage with fewer but longer sessions, or by allowing more than one session per act. With a novel of any length, divide the number of chapters by five (or so) and apply the same principle of reviewing a sizeable section of the text in one session.

If you are desperately short of time to revise and you need to re-visit a text in one sitting only, go straight to the end of the whole text and concentrate on reflecting on the final outcomes and what caused them.

Remember that there may be a contrast of size in your pair of exam texts. For example, you may be studying a 200-page novel and a two-act play. You must give them equal revision time – the questions on each will take equal time in the exam and will carry equal marks.

The exam requires you to manage your time effectively, and so does your revision.

The importance of English writing skills

The quality of your writing skills plays a significant part in your English Literature performance. Good control of your expression gets the examiner on your side and features as part of the overall judgement of your work.

In English Literature, it will be an advantage if you:

- ♣ communicate clearly
- ♣ organise your ideas into sentences, paragraphs and whole responses
- ♣ use a range of sentence structures effectively
- ♣ use a wide vocabulary
- ♣ use the grammar of standard English
- ♣ use accurate spelling and punctuation
- ♣ present work neatly and clearly.

Most important of all, **your writing should have a sense of purpose – in other words, answer the question as set.** Do not repeat the essay you wrote in the mock exam on last year's paper, and do not offload thoughtlessly everything you know about your set texts.

Knowledge and understanding

You will need to have a good working knowledge of the plot for each text you are studying, but you will not gain any great credit for writing it down in the exam. Your knowledge of the general outline of the story and your more detailed knowledge of characters and events must underpin your deeper understanding. Knowing that Mr Ormerod is the name of the shopkeeper in *Anita and Me* is only useful if you are able to fit him in to your understanding of Anita's childhood and the life of Tollington in the 1960s.

You need to be able to choose and use the right details from your texts according to the question you are answering. You need to discuss and interpret the underlying or deeper meaning of what you have read.

Mr Ormerod the shopkeeper plays a significant role in *Anita and Me* because it is his shop that Anita and Meena steal from. You would be right to say that he is therefore involved in key incidents in Anita's early life and the way she learns right from wrong. However, the reader also learns about Mr Ormerod – how all is not as it seems, namely that the man who claims to be a Christian has some fairly dubious moral attitudes. You might be capable of drawing out an idea that the author intended from your reading, e.g. children learn as they go through life that, shocking though it may seem, adults do not live up to the high standards that they claim for themselves.

If you can discuss ideas like these with some confidence while keeping close to the details of the text, you will be meeting some of the requirements of the mark scheme at the higher grades.

Style and structure

Being so involved in a story or sympathising with a character so much that you cannot put a book down is the level of reader engagement that writers must dream of! However, studying a book invites an extra dimension of response from a reader – an appreciation of the writer and the skills and techniques that he or she has employed. Put at its simplest, **style is the words on the page, and structure is the way the text is organised.** All writers start with a blank piece of paper and have to decide on a beginning, a middle and an end, which words are best for the occasion and, if you like, which order to put them in!

The quickest way to raise your awareness of style is to witness an obvious contrast between two very short prose extracts:

> The door opened, and a thick-set, heavy-looking young man entered, with the flushed face and the gratuitously elated bearing which mark the first stage of intoxication. It was Dunsey, and at the sight of him Godfrey's face parted with some of its gloom to take on the more active expression of hatred. The handsome brown spaniel that lay on the hearth retreated under the chair in the chimney-corner.
>
> 'Well, Master Godfrey, what do you want with me?' said Dunsey, in a mocking tone. 'You're my elders and betters, you know; I was obliged to come when you sent for me.'
>
> (from *Silas Marner* by George Eliot)

'We charged through on our bikes. Bikes became important, our horses. We galloped through the garage yards and made it to the other side. I tied a rope to the handlebars and hitched my bike to a pole whenever I got off it. We parked our bikes on verges so they could graze. The rope got caught between the spokes of the front wheel; I went over the handlebars, straight over. It was over before I knew. The bike was on top of me. I was alone. I was okay. I wasn't even cut. We charged into the garages –

Woo wooo wooo wooo wooo wooo wooo!

and the garages captured our noise and made it bigger and grown-up. We escaped out the other end, out onto the street and back for a second attack.

(from *Paddy Clarke Ha Ha Ha* by Roddy Doyle)

Look at these two passages and find as many differences as you can in the way the writers use words and sentences. From the limited evidence, explain the reasons behind these differences.

In good writing, style is always very closely linked to the content, as well as the history and culture of the text.

In prose, style is associated with the narrator and directly with the words on the page; in drama, you can concentrate more on character, performance, dramatic effects and dramatic signals. The whole of *A View From The Bridge* by Arthur Miller takes place in (or next to) a New York tenement building. It is meant to be a claustrophobic setting and an increasingly tense atmosphere; the overcrowded living conditions are present on stage and also in the words and actions of the characters as a tragic situation unfolds. Call it style or call it stagecraft, the playwright initially through the text (and then the director and actors) is responsible for the effectiveness of the drama.

The structure of a novel or play can stand out as particularly important in some cases. Several texts end where they begin, which is an especially effective structure. *A View From The Bridge* begins and ends with Alfieri commenting on the action of the play; likewise *Under Milk Wood*, with the First Voice describing the village of Llaruggeb in the early morning, then at night; in *Of Mice and Men* Lennie dies at the spot where he and George have discussed their dream at the start of the novel. Elsewhere, *Stone Cold* is characterised by short 'spoken' accounts from Link, interspersed by the ominous Daily Routine Orders, while *Anita and Me* follows a recognisably autobiographical form, ending with Meena going to grammar school and a fairly blunt closure of her relationship with Anita.

Shakespeare's five-act classical structure really demands a book of its own – but be reassured that at GCSE it is perfectly satisfactory (and more!) to respond to the parallels, the sub-plots, the ironies, the outcomes as they affect the characters. What you should be aware of are the critical scenes that typically punctuate a Shakespeare play, such as the trial of Shylock at the climax of *The Merchant of Venice*.

Inevitably, the shape of a novel or play will be part of its meaning and effect, so regard it as part of your continuing investigation as a student. Right through the grade descriptions (see page 13) there are references to style and structure. **Candidates are encouraged to show how different aspects of style combine to create effects (e.g. changes in mood and atmosphere) and to show how meanings and ideas are conveyed through language, structure and form. The best candidates are expected to be able to explore and analyse style and structure.**

Including background information

Under the name of social, historical and cultural contexts, this is something that is often misunderstood. It is not an essential component of an essay in literature nowadays, but it can be a useful feature in a good quality answer, if, and only if, comments are connected to an understanding of the text. For example, in *To Kill A Mockingbird*, it would be highly appropriate – to show an understanding of Maycomb in the early 20th century – to explain the context for the treatment of Black Americans in general, and Tom Robinson in particular.

When writing about *An Inspector Calls*, you would have a golden opportunity to probe the issue of social responsibility in Britain well beyond the Birling family. Less obviously, in studying *The Tempest*, you might link attitudes to the supernatural and the sub-human to Elizabethan exploration, and the fear and thrill of the unknown. **Whatever your text, do not miss an opportunity to look outwards to connected, wider issues, but do not let a consideration of them lead you away from your response to the text itself.**

Exam essentials

- Divide your time wisely between each question on the paper. Sort all of your questions quickly at the start of the exam. Let your subconscious mind do some work.
- Answer the question – do the task as set.
- Start at the sharp end – first impressions are vital. Think before you start.
- Give the examiner something positive to tick in the first sentence.
- Make the examiner think 'high grade?' after the first paragraph.
- Get the writer into your essay early on – see the writer as part of the discussion.
- Make your quotations short, frequent and integrated. The standard length of quote should be the 'phrase', i.e. less than a full sentence. However, the 'single word' quote may be appropriate and so might a whole sentence occasionally.
- Echo (or refer back to) the question in every paragraph. Often, one word will do it. If none of your paragraphs ties in with the question, then you have drifted away. If so, don't panic, but return to the trail promptly.
- Get to the heart of the text/character at the start of each question. Have an enthusiasm and respect for each text.
- A developed overview of each text should be a priority, however localised the extract you are working with. Don't leave the exam regretting missed opportunities to discuss key meanings of the texts – it's your chance. Make your essay work on the level of ideas as well as character/plot/situation.
- With extract questions particularly, don't meander loosely through the text – look at the outcomes from the extract, get them at or near the top of the essay, and pull the arguments together with good selection and highlighting.
- Manipulate language in your essay, modifying as you proceed rather than crossing out words and phrases. Crossings-out will betray indecision, while skilful manoeuvring will reflect well on you. It's often just an attitude of mind.
- The key unit of meaning is the sentence – if your sentences are controlled and purposeful, you stand a chance. If they are not, you are seriously compromised.
- Paragraphs are also important – they usually reflect the level of organisation in an essay. No or few paragraphs, or short paragraphs, normally betray problems with the authority and control of an argument. Use a paragraph for a definite purpose – say, discussing a character at a particular moment.
- Your conclusion, remember, came at the start of the essay! If you possibly can, end your essay with something consciously saved from earlier.
- Do not overrun your time on any question!

Look at the exemplar responses later in this guide for an illustration of some of the features mentioned above.

Shakespeare: verse and prose

As all candidates in England, and many in Wales, study one of Shakespeare's plays for coursework or the exam, here is an explanation as to how his dramatic language works.

Shakespeare's plays are predominantly written in verse, which is a convention, just as all of the plays are written in five acts. Verse, of course, is not how people spoke in reality but it acts as a distinction from prose, in the way that standard English is different from dialect. So, if you like, Shakespeare's verse is (more) formal and prose is informal.

Iambic pentameter is the standard verse form and is known as blank verse, very largely unrhymed. At its purest, it has, for each line, a regular musical rhythm (five alternating unstressed and stressed beats) and therefore a regular length (ten syllables). Even in his earliest, least sophisticated plays, Shakespeare avoided writing his verse with too predictable a pattern, but as he became more experienced he learned how to manipulate the verse form to maximum effect, merging recognisable rhythms of speech into the underlying pattern. So, for instance, you may have lines of nine, eleven or twelve syllables and you may have irregular patterns of stresses totalling more than five or less than five, but overall you will still be able to 'hear' the iambic pentameter line. By avoiding a monotonous beat, Shakespeare was able to represent a spectrum of moods and emotions and to create an individual 'voice' for each of his characters.

So, verse within the world of the Shakespearean play is appropriate for most occasions – for characters with status (from royalty down to high-ranking soldiers and officials) and for those who interact with them, e.g. servants who would have to speak 'proper' to their superiors. However, prose has its place too, extending further the range of voices and widening the spectrum of social types. 'Lowlifes' would probably only speak prose (street-language), but potentially all of the others would be able to interchange between verse and prose, depending on who they were talking to and why. Typically, speech/dialogue that is conspiratorial, very informal, bawdy, disrespectful or casual is presented in prose.

In short, you do not need to know about the technical aspects of verse, but it is very useful to know the broad differences between the verse and the prose in Shakespeare's plays.

Making the grade in the English Literature exam

In the English Literature exam, you will be graded according to your knowledge and understanding of texts, your ability to explore the language, the structure and the form of texts, and the way you communicate your response to a question or task. (In the Specification B exam, the quality of your work in comparing texts will also count towards your grade.)

G > F > E

You need to have a sound general understanding of your texts. You need to be reasonably clear about what happens in them and be able to pick out important details.

At Grade E, you should be able to:
- ♣ select relevant parts of the story clearly and efficiently
- ♣ comment on the skills of writers
- ♣ focus on the question set, giving opinions and backing them up with detail
- ♣ develop some points of comparison (Specification B exam).

E > D > C

You need to make sensible, detailed responses to the text(s), referring to the language, the structure and the themes.

At Grade C, you should be able to:
- ♣ make detailed references to the texts and explore the deeper meanings
- ♣ develop discussion of characters and relationships
- ♣ show understanding of the background of texts
- ♣ sustain a character's viewpoint (empathy)
- ♣ explore connections and comparisons (Specification B exam).

C > B > A > A*

You need to develop your ideas perceptively and confidently, with subtlety and precision. You must explore and interpret independently and with individuality.

At Grade A/A*, you should be able to:
- ♣ focus well on key areas of text, including the complex parts
- ♣ discuss texts in relation to their social, historical and cultural backgrounds
- ♣ analyse features of the style and technique of writers
- ♣ explore relationships and comparisons confidently, cross-referencing well-chosen points of detail with equally well-chosen comments (Specification B exam).

Mind Maps

Before we go on to consider extended writing on a set text, it's worth looking at mind maps.

Nobody's brain works in the same way or has the same strengths and weaknesses. Some people think in logical, bullet-pointed steps but other learners find this difficult. You will probably know by now what kind of a learner you are but, if not, just consider whether you find it easier to remember words, images, music or patterns. If, like 80% of us, the answer is images or patterns, then mind maps are for you.

Mind maps are a reasonably new way of organising your writing. Because they flow from the centre outwards, they naturally follow the connections and pathways that your brain makes. The main ideas form four or five central branches (yes, like a tree), which expand and develop, spreading outwards (yes, like twigs).

Although mind maps are very personal to their designers, there are a few basic rules that you need to follow in order to make your map work for you:

♠ Use either capital or lower case letters. Don't mix both.
♠ Write on the lines, not at the end of them (like a spider diagram).
♠ Try to use no more than two or three words on a line.
♠ Make the branches near the centre thick, gradually thinning as they radiate outwards, following your thoughts.
♠ Use colour, and try to make it relevant (e.g. red for Curley's wife).
♠ Use images instead of (or as well as) words whenever possible, and try to keep the images relevant or important to you (e.g. a tea towel for Beatrice in *A View From The Bridge* to highlight her domesticity).

Mind maps can be used in a variety of ways: they are great for revision, and also for planning essays at speed in exam conditions.

Before the exam

The very act of designing them, thinking of appropriate images, colours or patterns, will help to anchor the information in your brain. Pin them up around the house: seeing them day in day out will help to make them second nature. You could make individual mind maps for each character, major relationship or theme. You could make them for the main settings or simply to help you remember the plot. They will be a lot easier to recall than pages and pages of notes.

In the exam

Obviously under exam conditions you'll probably have to forgo the colour and images in favour of speed, but the same principle of central branches radiating outwards can be very useful when planning your essay questions in your Literature exam. Think of each main branch as a paragraph, and the smaller 'twigs' as the points you need to include in that paragraph. You can go back and forth between branches as many times as you like, building up your plan as your thoughts develop. This method is a lot more natural than trying to force your brain to write an orderly, formal list, especially in potentially stressful situations.

If you've never tried mind maps before, give them a go. Start off with something really simple: yourself as the central image and your hobbies, family, friends etc. radiating outwards. This should show you how easy it is to record your thoughts in this way. Don't forget your images and colour! Then try and replicate your map an hour or two later. You'll be surprised by how much you remember.

This is an example of a mind map on the set drama text *A View From The Bridge*.

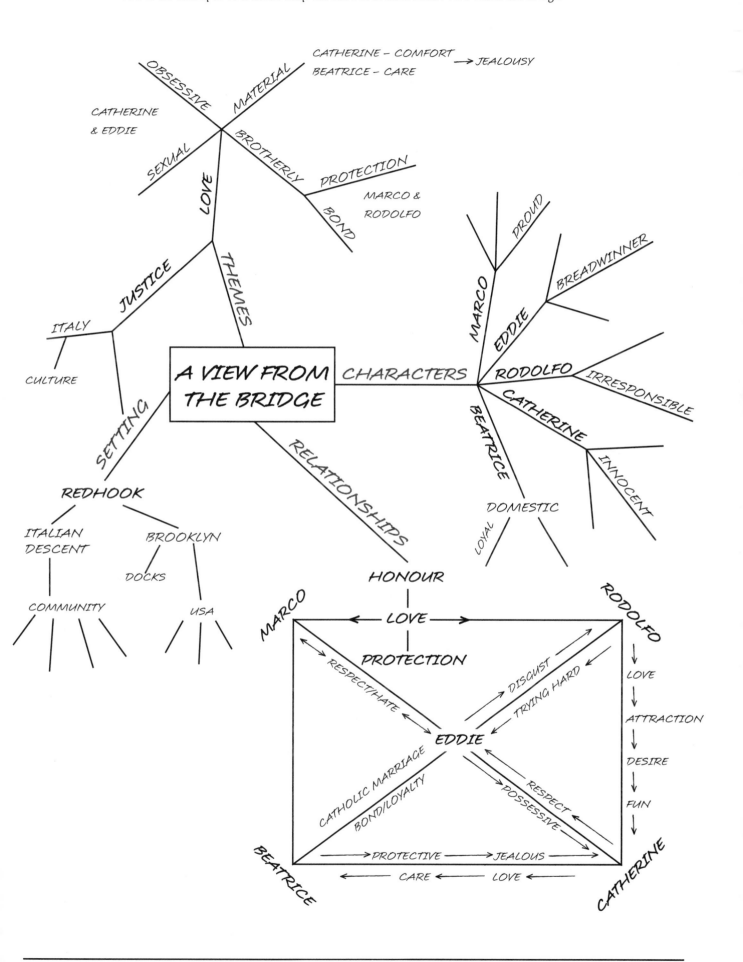

Specification A – Questions on an extract

Prose and drama

Below you will find a range of question types on extracts in Specification A. You will see that there is more support given in the Foundation tier, where the question is normally divided into two parts. During your revision you should attempt to apply these question types to your own set texts and write at least one full answer.

FOUNDATION TIER

♣ i) What thoughts and feelings do you have when you read this extract?
   ii) Choose parts of the extract that you find particularly effective in creating the thoughts and feelings and write about them, explaining why you find them effective.

♣ i) What are your thoughts and feelings about X (a character) here?
   ii) What are your thoughts and feelings about Y (the other character) here?

♣ i) What impressions of X do you have when you read this extract?
   ii) Choose parts of the extract that you find particularly effective in creating these impressions and write about them, explaining why you find them effective.

♣ i) What do you think about the way X (a character) speaks and behaves here?
   ii) What do you think of the way Y (the other character) speaks and behaves here?

♣ i) What do you think of the way X (a character) speaks and behaves here?
   ii) How do you think an audience would respond to this part of the play?

HIGHER TIER

♣ With close reference to the extract, show how the writer creates mood and atmosphere.

♣ Look closely at how X speaks and behaves here. What does it reveal about his/her character?

♣ With close reference to the extract, show how the writer suggests X's feelings here.

♣ Look closely at the way X speaks and behaves here. What does it reveal about his/her state of mind at this point of the novel?

♣ Look closely at how X and Y are presented here. How may the way they are presented affect an audience's attitudes towards each character?

♣ Look closely at how X and Y speak and behave here. What does it reveal about their relationship?

♣ Look closely at how X and Y speak and behave here? What does it reveal about each character?

♣ Look closely at how the characters speak and behave here. How does the way they speak and behave create mood and atmosphere for an audience?

Higher tier question (*To Kill A Mockingbird*)

Here is an extract from *To Kill a Mockingbird* by Harper Lee, together with a question for you to consider. Whether or not you are actually studying this novel, you might choose to annotate this extract. You could use the essay response on the next page as a source for your notes.

Read the extract. Then answer the following question:

> With close reference to the extract, show how Harper Lee creates mood and atmosphere.

I pulled him down beside me on the cot. I tried to reason with him. "Mr Nathan's gonna find 'em in the morning, Jem. He knows you lost 'em. When he shows 'em to Atticus it'll be pretty bad, that's all there is to it. Go 'n back to bed."

"That's what I know," said Jem. "That's why I'm goin' after 'em."

I began to feel sick. Going back to that place by himself – I remembered Miss Stephanie; Mr Nathan had the other barrel waiting for the next sound he heard, be it nigger, dog … Jem knew that better than I.

I was desperate. "Look, it ain't worth it, Jem. A lickin' hurts but it doesn't last. You'll get your head shot off, Jem. Please …"

He blew out his breath patiently. "I-it's like this, Scout," he muttered. "Atticus ain't ever whipped me since I can remember. I wanta keep it that way."

This was a thought. It seemed that Atticus threatened us every other day. "You mean he's never caught you at anything."

"Maybe so, but – I just wanta keep it that way, Scout. We shouldn'a done that tonight, Scout."

It was then, I suppose, that Jem and I first began to part company. Sometimes I did not understand him, but my periods of bewilderment were short-lived. This was beyond me. "Please," I pleaded, "can'tcha just think about it for a minute – by yourself on that place – "

"Shut up!"

"It's not like he'd never speak to you again or somethin' … I'm gonna wake him up, Jem, I swear I am – "

Jem grabbed my pyjama collar and wrenched it tight. "Then I'm going' with you – "I choked.

"No you ain't, you'll just make noise."

It was no use. I unlatched the back door and held it while he crept down the steps. It must have been two o'clock. The moon was setting and the lattice-work shadows were fading into fuzzy nothingness. Jem's white shirt-tail dipped and bobbed like a small ghost dancing away to escape the coming morning. A faint breeze stirred and cooled the sweat running down my sides.

He went the back way, through Deer's Pasture, across the schoolyard and around to the fence, I thought – at least that was the way he was headed. It would take longer, so it was not time to worry yet. I waited until it was time to worry and listened for Mr Radley's shotgun. Then I thought I heard the back fence squeak. It was wishful thinking.

Then I heard Atticus cough. I held my breath. Sometimes when we made a midnight pilgrimage to the bathroom, we would find him reading. He said he often woke up during the night, checked on us, and read himself back to sleep. I waited for his light to go on, straining my eyes to see it flood the hall. It stayed off, and I breathed again.

The night-crawlers had retired, but ripe chinaberries drummed on the roof when the wind stirred, and the darkness was desolate with the barking of distant dogs.

There he was, returning to me. His white shirt bobbed over the back fence and slowly grew larger. He came up the back steps, latched the door behind him, and sat down on this cot. Wordlessly, he held up his pants. He lay down, and for a while I heard his cot trembling. Soon he was still. I did not hear him stir again.

Student response

As soon as the extract begins, Harper Lee creates a tense atmosphere by using words which detail "strained" actions or intentions, and thus showing how Scout's resistance is already futile: "pulled" "tried". This sense of futility and growing tension is increased when Scout, in trying to reason with Jem and send him off going back only serves to justify why Jem is going in the first place. Jem's speech is slow and firm, in uncompromising terms.

> **Excellent focus on the details of the extract**

"That's what I know," said Jem. "That's why I'm goin' after 'em."

This statement of intent alone sounds menacing, and the growing sense of danger and certainty is fuelled when Lee simply writes, "I began to feel sick". The simplicity of the language allows the reader to use his/her information (and knowledge of previous goings on) to anticipate what shall happen, and also to fearfully consider the possibilities.

> **Prepared to explore ideas and sustain points**

She makes the mood more determined and focused, but also much more taut and tense by counter-acting Scout's pleading ("Please …") with sharp tenseness from Jem: "Shut up!"

Scout's language becomes more rambling and desperate, which again darkens the atmosphere, and then Lee intensifies the mood by including a violent physical action, with very violent physical words:

> **Double-edged moods – risking complexity!**

"Jem grabbed my pyjama collar and wrenched it tight. 'Then I'm goin' with you – ' I choked. "

Words like "wrenched" and "choked" imply turmoil but also decisive action. However Lee brings a more eerie, uncomfortable tone to the atmosphere as the two children move outside, by using death-associated words ("like small ghost") together with faintly disturbing words ("drain", "bobbed"). We know that Scout is nervous, and this increases the tension and suspense.

> **Impressive range of vocabulary**

"A faint breeze … cooled the sweat running down my sides."

The feeling of tension is subtly maintained as Scout continues to wait for Jem, and her thoughts (already diverging) still have sudden reminders of danger.

"It was wishful thinking" … "I breathed again".

This implies that her breath has been held and that she is held in anticipation. Although Jem returns safely, Lee reminds us of the danger involved in his mission, by using words implying "shaky" movements or secretive, traumatised feelings:

> **So closely tracked!**

"Wordlessly … I heard his cot trembling".

Commentary

This is a quality answer to a Higher tier extract question. The student goes straight into a detailed response with good focus on language. It is a full and closely analytical piece which is really alert to the style of the text.

Extended writing on a set text

Prose (Specification A) and Drama (Specifications A & B)

Here is an extensive list of question types for the essay and empathy tasks from past and specimen WJEC English Literature papers. Nearly all of the questions are interchangeable between prose and drama, but your answers should reflect whether it is a novel you are writing about or a play.

Foundation tier questions often come with the support of bullet points, as illustrated below. Characters and relationships feature regularly in the questions.

Higher tier questions are sometimes the same 'core' questions, but without the bullet points for support. Other Higher tier questions focus on the *presentation* of characters, i.e. the way the writer presents the character. Some questions concentrate on the themes, style and structure of novels and plays. There are a few questions that are specific to certain texts, such as: To what extent is X an effective title to the novel/play? You would not expect this type of question for a text whose title is the name of the main character, e.g. *Macbeth*.

Chief examiners are always looking for new and imaginative questions, so you too should be alert to all possibilities. But, rest assured, you will not be set trick questions.

FOUNDATION TIER

♣ Write about the relationship between X and Y and how it is presented at different points in the novel/play.
Think about:
- their first meeting
- X's feelings about Y
- Y's relationship with X
- the end of the novel/play.

♣ Imagine you are X . At the end of the story you think over what has happened. Write down your thoughts and feelings. Remember how X would speak when you write your answer.
You may wish to think about:
- your relationship with Y
- your reasons for…
- what happens at the end of the story.

♣ Write about your impressions of one or two of the following relationships that the writer presents in the novel/play.
(List of relationships to choose from)

♣ What do you think about the ending of the novel/play?
Think about:
- what happens
- what it shows about the different characters
- its mood and atmosphere
- how it brings the novel/play to an end.

♣ What do you think of X?
Think about:
- his/her first appearance
- his/her relationship with Y
- the way he/she speaks and behaves
- his/her importance to the novel/play as a whole.

♣ To what extent does the opening of the novel/play prepare the reader/audience for later events?
Think about:
- what happens in this part of the novel/play
- where this part of the novel/play takes place
- what we learn about the relationship between X and Y
- how later events link in with this opening.

♣ For which character do you have most sympathy? Give reasons for what you say and remember to support your answer with reference to the text.

♣ (Drama only) Imagine you have been asked to give advice to the actor playing X. Suggest how he/she should present the character to an audience in two or three different parts of the play.
Think about:
- X's relationships with other characters
- X's importance in the play
- how you think the audience may respond to X.

♣ Why do you think X (novel/play) is still popular today, at the beginning of the 21st century? Remember to support your answer with close reference to the text.
Think about:
- what happens
- the way the characters speak and behave
- the messages of the novel/play
- what makes the novel/play exciting and dramatic for a reader/audience.

♣ What do you learn about X (theme/place/character) in the novel/play? Remember to refer closely to the text in your answer.

♣ Who do you think is most responsible for...? Give reasons for what you say and remember to support your answer with reference to the text.

In your revision period, make sure you engage fully with as many of these question types as possible. You should attempt to write responses that are about three sides of A4 paper in length, even if at first they take you longer than the recommended time. As you get close to the exam, test yourself against the clock.

HIGHER TIER

♣ Write about the relationship between X and Y and how it is presented.

♣ Imagine you are X. At the end of the story you think over what has happened. Write down your thoughts and feelings. Remember how X would speak when you write your answer.

♦ At the beginning of the novel/play X is described as... Show how and why X's attitude changes as the story develops.

♦ Write about the presentation of X (theme) in the novel/play.

♦ Write about the presentation of one of the relationships and its importance to the text as a whole.

♦ Imagine you are X. Some years later you tell your story up to the point when... Remember how X would speak when you write your answer.

♦ Write about the character of X and the way he/she is presented.

♦ To what extent does the opening of the novel/play prepare the reader/audience for later events?

♦ To what extent do you find X an effective title for the play?

♦ Explain how the writer makes the reader/audience sympathise with X.

♦ For which character do you have most sympathy? Show how the writer's presentation of the character affects your responses to him/her.

♦ Write about the relationship between X and Y and how it is presented at different points of the novel/play.

♦ What is the importance of X (theme, place, character) to the novel/play as a whole?

♦ Why do you think X (novel/play) is still popular today, at the beginning of the 21st century?

♦ Why did...? Remember to support your answer with close reference to the text.

Tackle some of these questions by writing a response of about three sides of A4 paper, but plan others as well, either on paper or 'in your head'. Do not shy away from any of the 'difficult' questions. Face up to how you would organise a full answer under pressure in the examination.

Extended writing question (Higher tier – *Blood Brothers*)

Here is a student response to the extended writing question on *Blood Brothers* by Willy Russell:

What is the importance of Linda to the play as a whole?

Student response

Good – straight into a double-edged view of the character

In the play Linda has always been a source of fun and comfort, but her desire to behave like this for both Mickey and Eddie eventually leads to their deaths.

We see from the beginning of the play that she is eager to protect Mickey. When Mickey faces being unfairly excluded from the game she is the only character who stands up for him. She stands up for him, reasoning with Sammy why Mickey should still be included. When things start to get more serious, Linda shouts, "Leave him alone" at Sammy, showing her persistence and determination in protecting Mickey. She threatens Sammy, using her mother's stolen cigarettes as a reason to get him into trouble. This situation surprises Sammy, as he is usually the dominant child. But the fact that Linda is willing to stand up for him shows she has brave qualities. The way she tries to protect Mickey is a pattern that will recur in their lives.

As well as being a source of protection, Linda is mischievous and daring. When suggesting throwing stones through people's windows, she shows she is leadership material as even her male friends weren't willing to suggest such a daring task. She dominates them, and this will lead to her being the one to dominate their feelings near the end of the play.

Linda is a very strong character, and shows no qualms in being outspoken. When teenagers, she regularly blatantly tells Mickey of her love for him, which nearly always works to embarrass him. After Mickey and Eddie's reunion, it starts to become more apparent to the audience that Eddie has romantic feelings for Linda, symbolised in dreamy glances at her and compliments. It has always been obvious to the audience, however, that Mickey had strong feelings for her, summarised by his embarrassment of his mother's teasing. When Eddie sings to Linda before he leaves for university, he is stating his feelings for her that he can't bring himself to verbalise. There is a sense of relief that Eddie is going away, or Linda would've faced the tough decision of whether to choose Mickey or Eddie as her partner. It is clear by now that she feels strongly for both of them.

After falling pregnant after already choosing Mickey, Linda marries him. This means she potentially has no choices to make between the boys now, and to a certain extent she has taken the easy way out. When Mickey is struggling for work, Linda remains her usual strong self, but her tough circumstances are making her weary. She has actually turned by circumstance into a younger version of Mrs Johnstone.

She continues to support Mickey as he battles through his drug addiction, encouraging him in lines such as "You don't need those Mickey". She is consistently Mickey's rock through his tough times, but the pressure she is facing takes its toll. She is drained and yearns for more. She knows the comfort she can seek from Eddie, so eventually gives in to temptation and starts an affair. The line "wonders what the price would be for letting the girl out" makes clear that although Linda seeks excitement, she isn't willing to face the consequences. When Mickey finds out about the affair, he is already jealous, and bitter feelings towards Eddie are pushed to the edge.

Direct approach, gaining credit with words, phrases and whole sentences

Wise overview!

Consistent sense of drama (audience)

Strength of vocabulary, including verbs

All of this makes Linda a very important character within the play. A pattern throughout Mickey's life is that he has always wanted what Eddie has. The only "possession" which was truly earned and is his own, was Linda. This is because ultimately Mickey's existence is built upon everything Eddie has ever given him. So when Mickey realises he has now even lost Linda to Eddie who already has everything he craves he is heartbroken. His anger, jealousy, bitterness and sadness at losing his beloved pushes him to ultimately end Eddie's and his own life. The character of Linda is the catalyst that determines the outcome of the tragic story.

> Still making new points

> Ends strongly

Commentary

This is a very well sustained essay with a confident overview. It is discursive and analytical throughout, and is full of excellent supportive detail. Consistently thoughtful.

Extended writing question (Higher tier – *Romeo and Juliet*)

Here is a student response to the extended writing question on *Romeo and Juliet* by William Shakespeare:

Imagine you are Benvolio. At the end of the play you think over all that has happened. Write down your thoughts and feelings.

Student response

> Impact of opening – clearly looking back realistically

I knew we shouldn't have made him go to that party. There was something wrong about it, right from the start when dear Mercutio started talking about the dream he had. There was something ominous about the way he told the speech, and even though it was funny at the time, looking back there was more to it than I realised. It started off light-heartedly with the description of Queen Mab's chariot, I think. Towards the end, I can only remember horrific images of fighting and war. The whole speech built up to a violent chaotic dark crescendo and paralleled the events that followed in a worryingly similar manner.

> Thoughtful character qualities – frustration, for instance

At the party itself nothing seemed out of the ordinary. Rosaline was there but I was pleased to notice that Romeo didn't seem to be dwelling on his former infatuation. Then towards the end of the night he disappeared. I saw him at the very end having what looked like urgent discussions with Capulet's servant. I thought it odd at the time, but didn't dwell on it. I was more concerned that he then disappeared again and wasn't seen by anyone until the next day. This must have been when he met Juliet Capulet. My poor cousin, first he is infatuated with the highly unsuitable Rosaline, then his first and "only love sprung" from his "only hate". How I didn't realise his situation, I'll never know. He's my cousin, we used to be so close.

The next I saw of him was in the street when I was trying to prevent Mercutio from provoking the Capulets. I'm not a coward, I'd just prefer to avoid the confrontation if possible. Prevention is better than cure, as everyone finally began to realise when it was too late. When Romeo arrived, Tybalt made a beeline for him. He must have seen Romeo at the party, or maybe he knew that a Montague had kissed a Capulet. I knew none of this at the time but something about Romeo was making his blood boil.

> The voice is always credible

When Mercutio was stabbed, I saw the light of common sense rush out of Romeo's eyes. He was determined and focused, Tybalt would not get away with this. The worst moment of my life was to follow. My cousin had murdered the man who had killed my best friend. As usual, I was there to pick up the pieces. I felt terrible telling the Prince what Romeo had done. In my mind, banishment was better than death, at least I may see Romeo again. But thinking back, maybe my actions were selfish. Romeo is still dead, and now Juliet is as well.

> Drama through powerful phrasing

> Strength of engagement

Although I know I'm not entirely to blame, I feel so guilty for contributing to this horrific tragedy. Although it is terrible to try and find the silver lining to this dark, dark cloud it is the only way I can deal with my grief. The family feud is now over. Thinking about it, it doesn't surprise me as the only person still adding fuel to the fire of hatred that burned in Verona between the Montagues and the Capulets was Tybalt. Now that fire is out and in its place will soon be two magnificent gold statues of Juliet Capulet and Romeo Montague, who through their death created love and peace in Verona. This thought is what keeps me going. It is a small, flickering light at the end of a long, dark tunnel.

> In tune with the emotional power of the play

Commentary

This is a super empathy response, with a wholly convincing voice and excellent incorporation of references to language, structure, characters and relationships.

Specification A – Responding to an 'unseen' poem

In the examination, spend about 30 minutes on this section. Think carefully about the poem before you write your answer.

Some advice from John Idris Jones, author of the poems 'First Day' and 'Elvis Presley'

Your task is to understand the poem thoroughly and then to communicate this understanding in your own words to the examiner. Don't be afraid of the examiner; treat him/her as a friend and write as fully and clearly as you can.

Firstly read the poem with an open, alert mind. Then, to help understanding, ask yourself some simple questions. Who is involved in the poem – the poet himself/herself only? Or is the poem about somebody else? Where is the poem set – the geographical location of the scenes or actions portrayed? And, when (what times of the day/week/year/period) are the events happening? And, what actions, scenes are being portrayed? Then go back to the poem and read it again, trying to answer the above questions as you go.

Do not rush to write but on the other hand do not spend too long thinking and not writing.

You only get marks for what you have put on the page. If there are parts of the poem you are unsure about, go back and read them again. You need to explain the poem: begin with a comment on the title and continue through the poem, line-by-line. If the poem is in stanzas (groups of lines) then write a paragraph on each. Aim to include at least one direct short quotation in each paragraph. After you have done this – which is the task of re-telling the poem in your own words – then think of analysing the poem. Look for the meaning behind the words – what the poet's attitude towards his subject really is. Is there an overall theme? Select words and phrases from different parts of the poem and say how they transmit the poem's deeper meaning.

Do not be pretentious. Do not write merely to please the examiner. Ask yourself: what effect does this poem have on me? Your task is to 'unpack' that. Stay close to the words on the page and do not make things up which are not there.

Now put this advice into practice. Work through the questions on the poems by John Idris Jones on the following pages. Practise using annotations to enhance the quality of your responses.

Foundation tier: 'First Day' by John Idris Jones

Write about the following poem and its effect on you.

You may wish to include some or all of these points:
- the poem's content
- the ideas the poet may have wanted us to think about
- the mood of the poem
- how it is written – words or phrases you find interesting, the way the poem is structured or organised, and so on
- your response to the poem.

First Day
I am teaching again.

Sitting on the edge of the table
I turn on the old tricks
Like a performing animal.

They call me Sir,
Go out and fetch me chalk,
And I hardly recognise myself.

Lunch-time, the talk in the staff-room
I recognise from past years,
Old attitudes, jokes, introductions.
Then I wander out into the sunlight
Where the boys play ball
And the sun glares off the tarmac.

A teacher beside me talks.
He has just applied for a job at ICI
After 30 years teaching.

He doesn't like this school either.

Please God do not leave chalk in my pockets too long.

John Idris Jones

Points to consider

Explain the title: 'First Day'. Where? At what?
This is a poem with a distinct mood or tone. What is it? Consider the word 'again' in the first line. 'And I hardly recognise myself' – what does that tell us? Where is the poem located? Does the poet like this place? When do the circumstances of the poem happen? How does 'a job at ICI' connect with '... too long' in the last line?

J.I.J.

Annotated poem: 'First Day' by John Idris Jones

Annotation in the examination should be quick and practical. It provides a visual check that you have something useful to say about each section of the poem. Make sure that you convert your annotations into points and comments in your exam response. The examiner won't see any of what you leave behind in your question paper booklet!

First Day

had left teaching but has now returned

I am teaching again.

same old routine — no thought

Sitting on the edge of the table
I turn on the old tricks
Like a performing animal.   *circus*

They call me Sir,
Go out and fetch me chalk,   *children are very obedient; out of character*
And I hardly recognise myself.

no change since he's been away

Lunch-time, the talk in the staff-room   *not joining in? just watching?*
I recognise from past years,
Old attitudes, jokes, introductions.   *long sentences — increases boredom*
Then I wander out into the sunlight
Where the boys play ball
And the sun glares off the tarmac.   *hard, bleak — no grass*

everyone shares the boredom with the job — everyone wants to leave

A teacher beside me talks.
He has just applied for a job at ICI   *industry? factory?*
After 30 years teaching.

He doesn't like this school either.

Please God do not leave chalk in my pockets too long.   *doesn't want to stay at the school for long — sick of teaching after only one day; dreads the idea of staying*

John Idris Jones

Student response

Sensible personal approach

"First Day" describes the poet's thoughts and feelings as he returns to teaching. From the title of the poem, the reader assumes that the poet is feeling nervous and anxious; however, this impression quickly changes as the poem begins. The opening line forces the reader to anxiously wait to hear how the poet feels about returning to work, "I am teaching again". There is no emotion connected to this statement and so the reader must continue to find out whether the poet thinks this is a good thing or not. It soon becomes obvious that this is not a good thing as far as the poet is concerned. He sees his teaching as a boring routine that he is over-familiar with, "I turn on the old tricks". This implies that he is not even thinking about how he is teaching or what he is saying to the students. He also sees himself as a circus animal that is merely there for the entertainment of others, "like a performing animal".

Building very clear, coherent comments

Although the children are very obedient to him, "they call me Sir, go out and fetch the chalk", he seems to be acting out of character, "I hardly recognise myself". This could mean that he is not used to ordering people around. This is obviously coupled with the fact that he has not been teaching for a while and he no longer thinks of himself as a teacher.

The next stanza contains very long sentences, which creates the impression that the time is going very slowly and the teacher is very bored. The conversation in the staff room also adds to this sense of boredom, "the talk in the staff room I recognise from past years, old attitudes, jokes, introductions". The poet seems to be disheartened by the fact that nothing seems to have changed while he's been away. "Then I wander out into the sunlight," implies that he is preoccupied and not really thinking about anything that is going on. He watches the "boys play ball" on the "tarmac" and this creates the impression that the school is very bleak. The boys are playing on a hard black surface rather than on lush green grass.

> Good on mood

The poet's feelings are shared by one of his colleagues, "He doesn't like this school either". The poet adds that this colleague has "just applied for a job at ICI". This means that he dislikes teaching so much that he has decided to leave. This could possibly remind the poet of the reasons why he left teaching in the first place and that returning was a big mistake.

> Tracks detail patiently

> Soundly expressed meaning

The final line is very bleak and the poet is obviously feeling a deep sense of despair, "Please God do not leave chalk in my pockets too long". This appeal implies that he doesn't want to stay in teaching any longer than is necessary.

Commentary

The response tracks the poem very well, from the title through to the poem's last lines. The annotating work on the previous page pays off, because the details picked out in annotation are used sensibly as part of a sustained and consistent view of the man in the poem. There may be more to draw out of the poem in terms of the deeper meanings of the man's situation, but his dissatisfaction with his return to teaching is clearly expressed in this very capable piece of writing. In a Foundation tier examination, this answer would surely gain full marks, meeting the criteria for a grade C with some ease.

Higher tier: 'Elvis Presley' by John Idris Jones

Write about the following poem and its effect on you.

You may wish to include some or all of these points:
- the poem's content
- the ideas the poet may have wanted us to think about
- the mood of the poem
- how it is written – words or phrases you find interesting, the way the poem is structured or organised, and so on
- your response to the poem.

The poem was written shortly after the death of the singer Elvis Presley in 1977.

Elvis Presley

Truck driver;
found dead in his bathroom by an aide
then buried in a mausoleum.

Truck driver;
his father a cotton worker.
A raw boy from the South,
the rhythms of interlaced thruways
and black night sounds
beating into his body.

There is a power which bubbles out of the earth
which was in his voice.
He could roar and whisper in the space of a second.
His voice was all that lived; the body was a puppet.

His father kept his books
describing his crazy wealth.
He had no tax accountant, no investments.
The simple boy had it all as cash in the bank
and a fleet of Cadillacs and other toys.

Truck driver,
with a voice like a twister
and a body owned by millions,
with too much money and too many fears.

And he died,
The King,
When his ordinary heart lost its beat.

John Idris Jones

Points to consider

The poem contains clear contrasts between the ordinary and the extraordinary −
discuss this and quote from the poem to support your view. What is a puppet? Why
is this image in the poem? Is the poet sympathetic to his subject? How does he see
Elvis Presley's life?

J.I.J.

Annotated poem: 'Elvis Presley' by John Idris Jones

Annotation in the examination should be quick and practical. It provides a visual
check that you have something useful to say about each section of the poem. Make
sure that you convert your annotations into points and comments in your exam
response. The examiner won't see any of what you leave behind in your question
paper booklet!

Elvis Presley

sharp contrast – contradiction

Truck driver;

clinical, harsh, unfeeling description of his death

found dead in his bathroom by an aide
then buried in a mausoleum.

Truck driver;

very ordinary upbringing – typical, like any boy from the south?

his father a cotton worker

unrefined/uncultured

A raw boy from the South,
the rhythms of interlaced thruways
and black night sounds

musical beat from noise of roads and the wilderness → cacophony not music

beating into his body.

There is a power which bubbles out of the earth
which was in his voice

natural talent – controlled/manipulated by other people?

He could roar and whisper in the space of a second.
His voice was all that lived; the body was a puppet.

cannot believe his son's success

His father kept his books
describing his crazy wealth.
He had no tax accountant, no investments.

no financial sense?

uneducated? The simple boy had it all in cash in the bank
and a fleet of Cadillacs and other toys.

doesn't know what to do with his money – wastes it – instead of helping his father?

Truck driver,
with a voice like a twister *natural but uncontrollable force*
and a body owned by millions, *fans*
with too much money and too many fears.

And he died,

contradiction again – extraordinary man died in a very ordinary way

The King,
When his ordinary heart lost its beat.

reference to his music

when he stopped performing he died?

John Idris Jones

Student's response

"Elvis Presley" describes how an ordinary "raw boy from the south" grew up to be one of the world's most famous singers and how he could never escape these humble roots. There is a stark contradiction in the opening lines which play on the reader's expectations. The juxtaposition of the words causes a sharp contrast in the reader's mind, "Truck driver; found dead in his bathroom by an aide". This is clearly a very unusual scene because truck drivers do not have "aides". The contrast continues as this "truck driver" was "buried in a mausoleum". This is a very grand burial for someone who appears to be so ordinary.

The poet describes how Elvis had a very ordinary upbringing, typical of any other boy raised in the southern states of the USA, "his father a cotton worker, a raw boy from the south". This also attempts to explain where Elvis' extraordinary talent comes from. His exceptional musical talent is derived from the cacophony of beats from the busy roads and the wilderness that surrounds his family home. This seems like a very strange source for his musical ability and again demonstrates the sharp contrast between the rawness of Elvis' up bringing and his royal or godly persona as a star.

Has the language/ vocabulary to make sharp observations

Quality comments piled up!

Always looking for alternatives and contrasts

The poet reinforces the idea that Elvis' talent is natural and this echoes the ideas in the previous stanza that his voice was something everyone was in awe of, "there is a power which bubbles out of the earth which was in his voice." However, although Elvis appeared to be in complete control of his talent, "he could roar and whisper in the space of a second", actually this is just an illusion. He was really manipulated and controlled by other people, "the body was a puppet".

The idea that Elvis was uncultured and uneducated is reinforced again, "the simple boy had it all in cash in the bank". He had no business sense and probably never imagined he would ever have so much money. This is supported by the fact that he bought "a fleet of Cadillacs and other toys" with the money because he simply did not know what else to do with it. This feeling is clearly supported by his father, who "kept his books describing his crazy wealth". However, there may also be the implication in this line that Elvis should have shared his money with his father instead of wasting it on cars and "toys" and this is why his father cannot believe how rich his son is.

It begins to become apparent that "Elvis", the "puppet" controlled by his management team and producers was an unstoppable force, "like a twister". But again the idea that Elvis himself is not in control of his own life is reinforced, "a body owned by millions". The tone of the poem changes dramatically here, "with too much money and too many fears". This "raw boy" with an incredible natural talent, is after all the same as everyone else and even all of his money cannot stop him feeling frightened.

The poem ends with another contradiction, "The King" died "when his ordinary heart lost its beat". This extraordinary man died in a very ordinary way. The idea that his heart lost its beat, has a clear connotation in that once Elvis lost his passion for his music he had nothing to live for.

Controlled expression supporting the clarity of the argument

Frequent incursions into the details of the poem

Ends with a comment that reflects the poignancy of the poem

Commentary

This response is very assured. The details of the poem are consistently handled with confidence and developed alongside far-reaching issues of how the talented, but overburdened, individual tries to handle fame and exploitation. Within the answer there are moments of tentativeness and moments of assertion, both kinds of comment appropriately employed. This is an impressive Higher tier response with definite A* qualities.

Specification A – Key notes on your set prose text

For best effect, write in small print and in note form on this page.

Title

Author

PLOT The main points of the story in sequence

KEY EVENTS The major situations and dramatic scenes of the text

Specification A – Key notes on your set prose text

For best effect, write in small print and in note form on this page.

Title

Author

MAJOR CHARACTERS
Points about the important characters and their roles in the text

MINOR CHARACTERS
Points about the less important characters and why they appear in the text

Specification A – Key notes on your set prose text

For best effect, write in small print and in note form on this page.

Title

Author

THEMES Ideas, topics and areas of discussion that run through the text

LANGUAGE AND STYLE Key details of the way the text is written

MOOD/ATMOSPHERE/SETTINGS General terms and ideas that describe and explain the characters' feelings and the reader's response at different stages of the text

CONTEXTS Relevant points about the background of the writer and the text

Specification A – Key notes on your set prose text

For best effect, write in small print and in note form on this page.

Title

Author

QUESTIONS
Collected from past papers and specimens

QUOTATIONS
Important phrases/sentences from the text that might be worth using in the exam

Specification B – Anthology

Use the Contents page of your Specification B Anthology to indicate if you have both read [✓] and studied [✓✓] each of the prose items and the poems. You could also link with arrows any items that have strong points of comparison and contrast.

Remember that from 2005 you will not be allowed to use your annotated copy of the Anthology in the exam, but you will be given a 'clean' copy at the start of the exam.

Specification B – Prose Anthology

Higher and Foundation tier questions – prose extract

The extract question on the Higher tier may be structured something like this:

> Read the extract on the opposite page and then answer the following question:
>
> How does X (the writer) present Y (character/place/theme) in this extract?
>
> Make sure you refer closely to the language used. (10)

The extract question on the Foundation tier may concentrate on characters and relationships, rather than the writer. It may also be supported by bullet points, as follows:

> Read the extract on the opposite page and then answer the following question:
>
> What are your thoughts and feelings about X and Y and their relationships in this extract?
>
> In your answer write about:
> * the way X and Y are described
> * the way X and Y speak and behave
> * the way the extract is written.
>
> Make sure you refer to the words and phrases used. (10)

Higher and Foundation tier questions – extended writing on prose

There will be a choice of 'extended writing' questions requiring comparison of stories from the Prose Anthology. Here are two common question types:

> Some of these stories involve some kind of disappointment for a character.
>
> Remind yourself of X (title). Compare this with another story that involves some kind of disappointment for a character.
>
> In your answer write about:
> * the disappointment in each story
> * how the character reacts to the disappointment in each case
> * which story deals with disappointment in a more interesting way in your opinion.
>
> Remember to refer to words and phrases in each story to support your answer. (20)

Choose two stories, selecting an interesting character from each.

Explain why you find each character interesting.

Remember to refer to words and phrases in each story to support your answer.   (20)

Note: One of the key distinctions between the tiers is the quality of comparison in students' answers. See the grade criteria on page 13 in relation to skills of comparison.

Specification B – Poetry Anthology

Higher and Foundation tier questions – poem/extract

The poetry question on the Higher tier may be structured something like this:

Read the poem/extract on the opposite page and then answer the following question:

How does X (the writer) present his/her ideas in this poem?

You may wish to think about:
- the choice of words
- the way images are used
- anything else you find of interest.   (10)

The Foundation tier poetry question may offer more specific support, as follows:

Read the poem/extract on the opposite page and then answer the following question:

How does the poet present his/her ideas on love in this poem?

In your answer make sure you cover:
- the way the poet uses images
- the way he/she makes you feel about love
- the way the poem is organised
- anything else you find of interest.   (10)

Higher and Foundation tier questions – extended writing on poetry

There will be a choice of 'extended writing' questions requiring comparison of poems/extracts from the Poetry Anthology. Here are two common question types. Similar levels of support are offered on each tier.
In the Higher tier, more emphasis may be placed on comparison:

X and Y (poets) present portraits of various people in their poems. Compare two poems, one by each poet, commenting on each poet's description of people.

In your answer, consider:
- each poet's choice of language in describing people
- how each poet makes the person individual
- the way each poem is organised and structured.   (20)

In the Foundation tier, there may be less emphasis on comparison:

> X (poet) often presents nature (including animals) in his/her poems. Choose two poems, and examine the ways in which he/she writes about nature.
>
> In your answer you may wish to write about the following:
> - the way nature is described in each poem
> - the way people are shown reacting to nature
> - the way people are shown affecting nature
> - words and phrases you find interesting
> - similarities and differences between the two poems. (20)

Prose – extract from *Extraordinary Little Cough* by Dylan Thomas

Read the extract below and the question plus response on the following page. To practise the skill of annotation, use points made in the answer to annotate the extract.

Three girls, all fair, came down the cliff-side arm in arm, dressed in short, white trousers. Their arms and legs and throats were brown as berries; I could see when they laughed that their teeth were very white; they stepped on to the beach, and Brazell and Skully stopped singing. Sidney smoothed his hair back, rose casually, put his hands in his pockets, and walked towards the girls, who now stood close together, gold and brown, admiring the sunset with little attention, patting their scarves, turning smiles on each other. He stood in front of them, grinned, and saluted: 'Hallo, Gwyneth! Do you remember me?'

'La-di-da!' whispered Dan at my side, and made a mock salute to George still peering at the retreating sea.

'Well, if this isn't a surprise!' said the tallest girl. With little studied movements of her hands, as though she were distributing flowers, she introduced Peggy and Jean.

Fat Peggy, I thought, too jolly for me, with hockey legs and tomboy crop, was the girl for Dan; Sidney's Gwyneth was a distinguished piece and quite sixteen, as immaculate and unapproachable as a girl in Ben Evans' stories; but Jean, shy and curly, with butter-coloured hair, was mine. Dan and I walked slowly to the girls.

I made up two remarks: 'Fair's fair, Sidney, no bigamy abroad,' and 'Sorry we couldn't arrange to have the sea in when you came.'

Jean smiled, wriggling her heel in the sand, and I raised my cap.

'Hallo!'

The cap dropped at her feet.

As I bent down, three lumps of sugar fell from my blazer pocket. 'I've been feeding a horse,' I said, and began to blush guiltily when all the girls laughed.

I could have swept the ground with my cap, kissed my hand gaily, called them señoritas, and made them smile without tolerance. Or I could have stayed at a distance, and this would have been better still, my hair blown in the wind, though there was no wind at all that evening, wrapped in mystery and staring at the sun, too aloof to speak to girls: but I knew that all the time my ears would have been burning, my stomach would have been as hollow and as full of voices as a shell. 'Speak to them quickly, before they go away!' a voice would have said insistently over the dramatic silence, as I stood like Valentino on the edge of the bright, invisible bull-ring of the sands. 'Isn't it lovely here!' I said.

I spoke to Jean alone; and this is love, I thought, as she nodded her head and swung her curls and said: 'It's nicer than Porthcawl.'

Extract question (Higher tier)

Read the extract on the opposite page and then answer the following question:

> How does Dylan Thomas present the girls and boys, and the way they react to each other, in this extract from *Extraordinary Little Cough*?
>
> Make sure you refer closely to the language used.

Student response

No wasted words

In this extract Dylan Thomas presents the boys as being rather shy towards the opposite sex, except Sidney who had met the girls before. They appear to be quite confident to start with as they go over to talk to the girls, "Dan and I walked slowly to the girls", but the adverb "slowly" indicates that they are in fact quite nervous and are giving themselves time to think about what they are going to say. The boy's shyness is apparent in the text when he drops the sugar lumps, which were probably brought to eat like sweets; "as I bent down, three lumps of sugar fell from my blazer pocket. 'I've been feeding the horse,' I said, and began to blush guiltily when all the girls laughed." The verb "blush" indicates his embarrassment of the situation. They are also presented as being quite poor with the quote as they have sugar lumps instead of sweets. The boys are also presented as being quite naïve in their attitude to love, "this is love,' I thought" as he believed the feeling she had towards her to be love although he had only met her a few minutes prior to this.

Full of the ironies and sensitivities of their behaviour – in tune!

The girls are presented as being very self-conscious, "with little studied movements of her hands" this indicates that the moves she made were carefully thought out showing their self-awareness. They believe they look elegant when doing this. The girls are also shown to be not as interested in the boys as they are with themselves. "I could have...made them smile without tolerance," the words "without tolerance" indicate that at that moment they were smiling out of kindness and just tolerating him, therefore showing they are not really attracted to him. The girls are also presented as being quite teasing, "as I stood like Valentino on the edge of the bright invisible bull-ring of the sands" this compares the boys' situation to that of Valentino at a bullring. It connotes the excitement and teasing of new relationships. He is the bullfighter waiting for the bull and the girls are the bull teasing him. Another way in which the boys are presented is to be very nervous again, "my stomach would have been as hollow and as full of voices as a shell" which indicates his nervousness by comparing what he's feeling to this, i.e. he has butterflies.

Understands the girls too!

Drawing out a subtle generalisation

Whole answer laced with key words and phrases

Commentary

This is a tightly argued piece with close language work of consistent quality. There is some mature observation of the characters and some precise quotations for supporting comments.

Extended writing question (Higher tier)

The extended writing question on the Higher tier may be structured something like this:

> Remind yourself of 'Snowdrops'. Compare this with another story that involves some kind of disappointment for a character.

Note that the story 'Tea in the Wendy House' will not appear in the 2005–2007 Prose Anthology.

Student response

Both of the stories 'Tea in the Wendy House' and 'Snowdrops' involve some kind of disappointment for a character. In 'Snowdrops' the character that suffers the disappointment is the boy (the main character). All the way through the story he looks up to his teacher and admires her. He sees her as a brave, heroic figure. However, at the end of the story he is disappointed when he sees his teacher break down with grief. The disappointment the character in 'Tea in the Wendy House' suffers is quite different. The character of Lynn is disappointed throughout the whole story, when she was younger she imagined life with a child, as a family would be happy and great. But as she grew up and became pregnant at a very young age she was disappointed, as this was not true. She feared she had ruined her chances in life and feared being trapped by her house and everything that comes with it, i.e. the family etc.

[margin note: Sets up a central comparison in a controlled, balanced manner]

The boy in 'Snowdrops' reacts to his disappointment by watching Miss Webster with fear and respect at the same time. This to him was the first tragedy he had seen and his whole faith in adults was shattered because his 'brave' teacher was crying and was not as brave as he had once thought. 'Miss Webster continued to cry aloud in the midst of the frightened children,' the adverb 'frightened' indicates that the children were scared of their first tragedy and were not so sure any more about what they had once believed, that adults did not cry or have emotions, they were just brave. The snowdrops are battling against the wind and shake a bit but 'straighten gallantly' afterwards, so in his eyes Miss Webster is battling against the grief and her tears are the equivalent to the snowdrops shaking, but he believes she will also 'straighten gallantly', i.e. pull herself together.

[margin note: Returns to the first texts and settles down to make pertinent points]

In 'Tea in the Wendy House', Lynn reacts to her disappointment with worry and fear. She is very worried about becoming like the previous owner of her new house, i.e. sad and alone, after having the baby. The walls in her house are blue indicating her sorrow (she's got the 'blues'). After the disappointment of being pregnant she is worried that Graham will feel the same disappointment and will leave her eventually.

[margin note: Less on return to second text, but balance is attempted]

In my opinion, 'Snowdrops' deals with disappointment in a more interesting way. I think this is because the view of disappointment from a child's perspective is very realistic and original, which makes it more interesting in my opinion.

[margin note: Coherent summing up]

Commentary

A very thoughtful answer that displays careful organisational skills – the element of comparison is comfortably handled, and comments are made with some authority. The response is succinct but shows regular evidence of mature understanding that merits a high grade.

Specification B – Key notes on your WJEC Prose Anthology

From 2005 you will not be allowed to take your annotated copy of the Anthology into the exam. You will, however, be given a 'clean' copy of the Anthology in the exam room.

For best effect, write in small print and in note form on this page.

INDIVIDUAL TEXTS
Key points about what is in the texts and how they are written

COMPARISONS
Key points that link the texts and that can be developed

Specification B – Key notes on your WJEC Poetry Anthology

From 2005 you will not be allowed to take your annotated copy of the Anthology into the exam. You will, however, be given a 'clean' copy of the Anthology in the exam room.

For best effect, write in small print and in note form on this page.

POEMS and POETS
Key points about what is in the poems and how they are written

COMPARISONS
Key points that link the poems and that can be developed

Specifications A and B – Key notes on your set drama text

For best effect, write in small print and in note form on this page.

Title

Author

PLOT The main points of the story in sequence

KEY EVENTS The major situations and dramatic scenes of the text

Specifications A and B – Key notes on your set drama text

For best effect, write in small print and in note form on this page.

Title

Author

MAJOR CHARACTERS
Points about the important characters and their roles in the text

MINOR CHARACTERS
Points about the less important characters and why they appear in the text

Specifications A and B – Key notes on your set drama text

For best effect, write in small print and in note form on this page.

Title

Author

THEMES Ideas, topics and areas of discussion that run through the text

LANGUAGE AND STYLE Key details of the way the text is written

MOOD/ATMOSPHERE/SETTINGS General terms and ideas that describe and explain the characters' feelings and the reader's response at different stages of the text

CONTEXTS Relevant points about the background of the writer and the text

Specifications A and B – Key notes on your set drama text

For best effect, write in small print and in note form on this page.

Title

Author

QUESTIONS
Collected from past papers and specimens

QUOTATIONS
Important phrases/sentences from the text that might be worth using in the exam

Tiers, grades and marks

Tiers – grades awarded

Foundation tier   G   F   E   D   C

Higher tier   D   C   B   A   A*

There is a 'safety net' of 'an allowed E' for candidates who narrowly miss a grade D on the Higher tier.

> You will not be entered for the Higher tier unless you are a clear C-grade candidate with a chance of a B grade.
>
> On the Higher tier:
> - ♣ There may be less support in the form of bullet points and other advice.
> - ♣ There is more emphasis on the higher level skills (e.g. the way the texts are written).
> - ♣ There may be more focus on the difficult parts of texts.
> - ♣ In the 'unseen' poetry section of Specification A, the poem may be more difficult.

Grades and marks

All tasks in the English Literature exam(s) are either marked out of 10 or out of 20. The relationship between grades and marks is different on the Higher tier from the Foundation tier.

Grade band	Foundation (/10) (/20)	Higher (/10) (/20)	Qualities in reading and writing
G/F	2–4 5–9	0–1 0–4	generalized; straightforward
E/D	5–7 10–14	2–4 5–9	clear; developing; supported
C/B	8–10 15–20	5–7 10–14	detailed; structured; sustained
A/A*		8–10 15–20	confident; subtle; precise